Customs Around the World

TRANSPORTATION
Around the World

by Lindsay Shaffer

PEBBLE
a capstone imprint

T0050822

Pebble Explore is published by Pebble, an imprint of Capstone.
1710 Roe Crest Drive
North Mankato, Minnesota 56003
www.capstonepub.com

Library of Congress Cataloging-in-Publication Data is available on the Library of Congress website.
ISBN: 978-1-9771-2376-3 (hardcover)
ISBN: 978-1-9771-2676-4 (paperback)
ISBN: 978-1-9771-2413-5 (eBook PDF)

Summary: Look both ways before you cross the street! A bus, car, or tuk tuk might be whizzing by! Find out how people around the world get around.

Image Credits
Alamy: imageBROKER, 21, Mike Goldwater, 19; Getty Images: NurPhoto/Contributor, 13; iStockphoto: wanderluster, 17; Shutterstock: Aleksandar Todorovic, 24-25, barteverett, 1, BrandonKleinVideo, 6, caminel, 26, G Allen Penton, 23, Hiromi Ito Ame, 18, I. Noyan Yilmaz, 20, Joseph Sohm, 10-11, lkoimages, 15, meunierd, 9, MVolodymyr, 28, phantomm, 12, QOcreative, 7, RickDeacon, 27, S-F, Cover, 8, Suparin, 5

Editorial Credits
Editor: Gena Chester; Designer: Julie Peters; Media Researcher: Jo Miller; Production Specialist: Spencer Rosio

Consultant Credits
Bryan K. Miller, PhD
Research Affiliate of Museum of Anthropological Archaeology
University of Michigan

Printed in the United States
PO117

TABLE OF CONTENTS

Travel Around the World 4

In the City 6

Animal Transport 16

In the Snow 20

In the Air 22

On the Water 26

Map 29

Glossary 30

Read More 31

Internet Sites 31

Index 32

Words in **bold** are in the glossary.

TRAVEL AROUND THE WORLD

Around the world, people need to get from place to place. They take short trips to work. They visit markets. Some take long trips. They visit family. All use many types of **transportation**.

In cities, people may ride buses or trains. Some drive cars. People in the **countryside** may ride horses. They may drive cars too.

People in Thailand
waiting for a bus

Water surrounds some towns.

People there use boats to travel.

How do you get from place to place?

IN THE CITY

Cities are busy places. Many people live close together. They need a lot of ways to get around. Trains can carry hundreds of people. Most run on a steel track. Some run underground.

The **subway** in New York City is a famous underground train system. Millions of people use it each day. Have you been on a train?

A subway train arrives at Penn Station in New York.

A maglev train in Shanghai, China

Shanghai, China, has the fastest train in the world. It's called a maglev train. The train uses magnets to lift into the air. Other magnets push and pull the train. It speeds up to 267 miles (430 kilometers) per hour! The ride is smooth and quiet.

Buses travel through cities and countrysides. Many people ride them daily. Double-decker buses zoom through the streets of London. People take them to work or school. They use them to go shopping. **Tourists** ride buses to see the city.

Double-decker buses
in London, England

A micro

Buses weave through the streets of Lima, Peru. The bus system is called *El Metropolitano*. The buses run along set **routes**. But they do not go all over the city. Many people take smaller buses. These are called micros. Some take vans called combis.

Does your family travel by car? In Los Angeles, California, many people drive cars. This causes a lot of **traffic**. People can spend hours stuck on the road!

People also use **rideshares** and taxis. Rideshares can be free or cost money. The cars are owned by the drivers. Taxi drivers use cars owned by a company. Rides with taxis always cost money. Using rideshares and taxis means fewer cars on the roads.

City streets are often jammed with cars and buses. Smaller types of transportation can move faster through traffic. In Thailand, tuk tuks are popular. Tuk tuks only have three wheels. They are open on each side. People take them through crowded streets.

A tuk tuk

A motorbike on a busy road in Lagos.

Many people around the world use motorbikes. These speedy bikes cost much less than cars. They are smaller than motorcycles. People take them through the busy streets of Lagos, Nigeria. People there even ride motorbike taxis!

Have you ever ridden your bike to school? People in Copenhagen, Denmark, do.

Copenhagen even has bicycle highways! People can rent bikes or electric scooters. This makes it easy to miss traffic. Scooters and bikes can zip past stopped cars.

ANIMAL TRANSPORT

Many people live far from cities. Some live on farms or ranches. Others live on mountains or in deserts. Some places have few roads. In places like these, people often ride animals.

In the U.S., some people work on cattle ranches. Cattle travel over miles of land. Ranchers ride horses to guide and lead cattle. Horses can go places cars cannot. They can walk in water. They can climb rocky ground. Have you ever ridden a horse?

In the mountains of Tibet, people use yaks. Yaks can carry heavy packs. Their strong backs can hold hundreds of pounds! They can walk long distances too. They help people carry supplies to mountain villages.

People in Somalia ride camels. These animals travel easily across the desert. They also help people move goods. Camels can carry over 200 pounds (91 kilograms)!

IN THE SNOW

In Antarctica, snow and ice cover the ground all year. The ice can be very thick. Sometimes it's over a mile deep! People use snowmobiles to get around. Snowmobiles can seat one or two people. Some can speed over 150 mph (241 kph)! Would you ride one?

A snowmobile in Antarctica

A dogsled team in Greenland

Winter in Greenland brings thick layers of ice and snow. Dogsleds help people get across the frozen land. **Mushers** attach their dogs to sleds using ropes. Then, they stand on the back of the sleds. They shout a **command**. The dogs take off, pulling the sleds behind them!

IN THE AIR

Have you flown in an airplane? Some planes carry hundreds of people! Others seat only a handful of people.

In Alaska, many people own planes. There are few roads for cars and buses. People fly planes to travel outside of town. The planes are small. Many can land on water!

A plane parked on water in Alaska

La Paz, Bolivia, rests in the mountains. Many people there ride cable cars. Cable cars cost less than buses. They carry people high above the ground to a city called El Alto. It takes 10 minutes to get there.

Cable cars traveling over La Paz

The cars hang from long steel cables. The cables move the cars forward. They are strung between tall poles. At each end, the cars arrive at stations. There, people get on and off.

ON THE WATER

Some places in the world are surrounded by water. Venice, Italy, is a city built on islands. Instead of roads, waterways called **canals** weave through the city. Long, thin boats help people get around. The boats are called gondolas.

Gondolas on a canal in Venice

A ferry in Sydney

A big river runs through the middle of Sydney, Australia. Many people travel over it. They take **ferries**. These big boats carry passengers on short trips. Some of them carry cars too. Would you like to travel by boat?

People use many types of transportation. This depends on where they live. Some people live in places that are hard to get to. They might use planes. Others ride animals. People in big cities take trains. What are your favorite ways to travel?

MAP

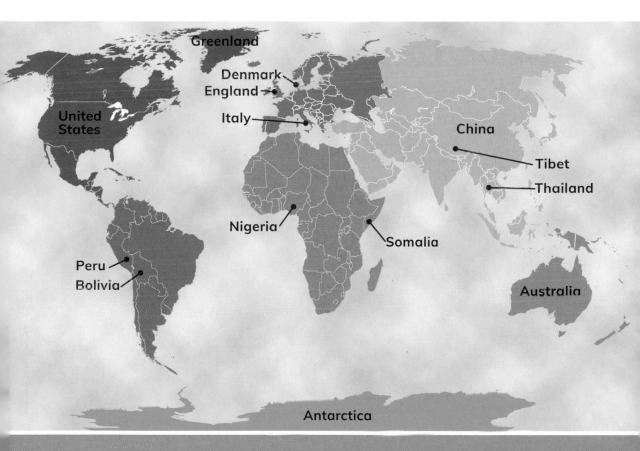

Greenland

Denmark

England

Italy

United States

China

Tibet

Thailand

Nigeria

Somalia

Peru

Bolivia

Australia

Antarctica

Around the world, there are many ways to travel. See which places were talked about in this book!

GLOSSARY

canal (kuh-NAL)—a channel of water dug across land; canals connect bodies of water

command (kuh-MAND)—a word that tells what to do

countryside (KUHN-tree-side)—land not in towns or cities

ferry (FAYR-ee)—a boat or ship that carries people across a stretch of water

musher (MUSH-uhr)—a person who travels over snow with a sled pulled by dogs

rideshare (RIDE-shayr)—a type of transportation where someone rides in a car that's being driven by the car's owner; ridesharing can cost money

route (ROUT)—a plan to get from one place to another

subway (SUHB-way)—a kind of train that runs under the ground

tourist (TOOR-ist)—a person who travels and visits places for fun

traffic (TRAF-ik)—vehicles that are moving on a road

transportation (transs-pur-TAY-shuhn)—a way to move from one place to another

READ MORE

Drane, Henrietta. *Around the World in 80 Ways.* New York: DK Publishing, 2018.

Hudak, Heather C. *Pathways Through Africa.* New York: Crabtree Publishing Company, 2019.

Meister, Cari. *Airplanes.* North Mankato, MN: Capstone Press, 2019.

INTERNET SITES

Amazing Transport
www.natgeokids.com/uk/kids-club/entertainment/books/amazing-transport/

Are We There Yet?: Adventures in South America
kids.nationalgeographic.com/videos/are-we-there-yet/are-we-there-yet-south-america/

Transportation
www.dkfindout.com/us/transportation/

INDEX

airplanes, 22, 28
Antarctica, 20
Australia, 27

bikes, 14
boats, 5, 26, 27
Bolivia, 24
buses, 4, 8, 9, 12, 22, 24

cable cars, 24–25
camels, 19
canals, 26
cars, 4, 10–11, 11, 12, 13, 14, 16, 22, 27
China, 7

Denmark, 14
dogsleds, 21

England, 8

ferries, 27

gondolas, 26
Greenland, 21

highways, 14
horses, 4, 16

Italy, 26

motorbikes, 13
motorcycles, 13

Nigeria, 13

Peru, 9

rideshares, 11
roads, 10–11, 11, 16, 22, 26
routes, 9

scooters, 14
snowmobiles, 20
Somalia, 19
subways, 6

taxis, 11, 13
Thailand, 12
Tibet, 18
traffic, 10, 12, 14
trains, 4, 6, 7, 28
tuk tuks, 12

United States, 6, 10, 16, 22

vans, 9

yaks, 18